Kevin Almighty

Bruce Dawe

Kevin Almighty

A verse play

PICARO PRESS

Kevin Almighty: A verse play
ISBN 978 1 921691 69 0
Copyright © text Bruce Dawe 2013

First published by Picaro Press 2013

This edition published 2015 by
Picaro Press – an imprint of
GINNINDERRA PRESS
PO Box 3461 Port Adelaide 5015 Australia
www.ginninderrapress.com.au

Cast of Characters

Ozzie Manning
Choir
Kevin Rudd
Speech-writer
Two Enemies
Journalist
Tony Abbott
Rock-and-Roll Duo
Joe Hockey
Malcolm Turnbull
Early August Blonde
Late August Brunette
September Redhead
Rowers
Pro-smoking Spruiker
John
Woman
Man
Green One
Green Two
Green Three
Bob
Attendant
Male Commentator One
Male Commentator Two
Male Commentator Three
Isabel
True Believer
Sam Spinmeister
Simon Breen

Act One

[Lights up. OZZIE MANNING is already sitting in his armchair, watching TV, facing audience, the usual newspaper draped over an armrest.]

OZZIE: Y'know, I thought there for a minute
I was havin' a dream of sorts and I was in it:
A dream of somethin' I saw some time ago
But, thinkin' about it again, I just dunno.

[OZZIE shakes his head, as if trying to wake up. Then he jabs a finger at his TV.]

There he is, right there! That Ruddy bloke,
Large as life right there on the idiot box.
I thought we'd seen the last of him, but (no joke!)
He's back again. The lot of 'em must've had rocks
In their heads to give him another go.
They sacked him once, and even this Party vote
You could hardly call overwhelming. Why didn't they give
Some other bugger a shot? Their bloody boat
Is as bodgie as that Tampa one, the Siev,
Leaking all over the place, with trouble below.

[Lights down on OZZIE, as he exits. Lights up on CHOIR, which enters singing joyfully.]

CHOIR: Kevin Rudd has risen today,
        Hallelujah!
And this time he's here to stay,
        Hallelujah!
Now he is once more the Boss,
        Hallelujah!
The prophet now redeeming loss,
        Hallelujah!

The media will sing his praise once more,
>Hallelujah!
And the Golden Age restore,
>Hallelujah!
North, south, east and west he's king,
>Hallelujah!
Tributes to his glory bring,
>Hallelujah!

[Exit CHOIR, still singing. Sign drops indicating THE LODGE. KEVIN is greeting all foreign ambassadors invited to a morning-tea party. They line up dutifully, one behind the other, all in dark suits.]

KEVIN *[shaking hands with each in turn]*: Good morning Jeff, say hello to President Obama for me Good morning Chen Yuming sorry about what I said in Copenhagen All the best to our friends in San Salvador I enjoyed my time there a couple of years ago How are our friends in Kiev? Give our best to Karmid Karzai All our best to our friends in Afghanistan and look after our solders Give my best to our friends in Skopje My very best to our friends in Seoul? Give my regards to all in Tehran It would be good to keep in contact giving the challenges we face And give my best to His Majesty and to the Labour government in Malta Say Hi to Xanana and give Kirsty a big kiss from me and that was a lovely visit to Indonesia Please tell SBY I appreciated it *Bonjour m'sieur* and *Arrividerci Roma*…

[Lights up again as KEVIN enters, smiling comfortably after morning tea with foreign ambassadors.]

KEVIN: While honoured by this reception
I must make *one* exception:
Before honour comes...
[*Bows head*]a deep humility
Before you all I stand,
Despite appearances, cap in hand,
For, from my cradle, my folks taught to me

[Ponders for a second.]

(Quoting St Peter 5, I think)
Whenever you find yourself on the brink
Of pride, stand back! All grace is to the humble.

So what if your enemy like a lion roars
With his tedious whys and heretofores?
Grace does not favour those who err and stumble.
[*Confidentially*]
My PM predecessor, you know,
Couldn't cut it, she had no 'glow',
Sounded like that schoolmarm we all used to hate,
With that voice of hers, lacking all verve,
You'd feel like you're getting a serve
And about to be put on detention again for being late.

[Enter a youngish SPEECH-WRITER for KEVIN, holding note-pad and biro.]

SPEECH-WRITER: I'm the latest speech-writer for Kevin,
It's an honour, a challenge, the lot!
I'm good at my job,
I'm ahead of the mob,
And I'm going to give it my very best shot, best shot;
I'll give it my very best shot!

He's hard to catch up with, is Kevin.
But I did catch him once on a plane
Which we shared with a crew
Of other speech-writers too,
And I'm hoping to meet him again, again,
I'm still hoping to meet him again.
Well, I wrote him in one week six speeches,
One for Brisbane and one for Moree.
One for Sydney, and Melbourne (he's so busy, you see)
And for Adelaide too; I was trembling with glee
So much that I could hardly tell Fosters from tea,
Couldn't hardly tell Fosters from tea!

Then I bought all the papers to follow the momentous event
And checked all the headlines to see how they went,
But bugger me dead, I shook my sad head,
For he never used *one*, that son-of-a-gun.
That part of my life was a big non-event,
A *momentously* big non-event!

[A thoughtful pause.]

An official told me back when I started
(The best piece of wisdom I was ever imparted):
'You're a 'snow-leopard', you know,
Their habitat's in the African snow…'
When I asked him to explain this peculiar distinction,
He smilingly said 'The snow-leopard up there
Is beautiful and rare,
But they're always at risk of extinction!'

[SPEECH-WRITER shrugs to audience. Dolefully exits.]

KEVIN: [*Struts a little, sending himself up.*]

>   Standing right where I am now
>   (A polished campaigner – and how!
>   Just so long as the light is shining directly on me).
>   I'm a performer who knows how to 'glib' it,
>   You'll never find me on the gibbet,
>   The Wonder from Eumundi is quicker that any old flea!
>   I live for the camera's enhancing stare,
>   For the constant flicker of crowd-scenes where
>   It's easier to forget about that other
>   World of meetings and men who'll smother
>   The drive and the drama, that illusion of speed,
>   Of meaning and purpose we all of us need.

[KEVIN consults his watch.]

>   Look, much as I like shooting the bull,
>   My working-day now's pretty full
>   Gotta zip… It's one of the burdens of being 'top dog'.
>   In this 24/7 business
>   You get used to these spells of dizziness;
>   How on earth did Howard fit in his 8 o'clock jog?

[Lights down as KEVIN exits. Lights up… A devotional hymn is softly played offstage. KEVIN is kneeling at his private altar, facing audience.]

>   Dear Lord, at Thy right hand I sit,
>   Of all the sons of men most fit
>   To rule in Parliament (and without),
>   Leaving News Limited in no doubt
>   (In spite of all their wicked sneers)
>   That I'll be here for three more years.
>   So, Lord, just as in ancient times
>   When your anointed suffered crimes,
>   You urged them frequently to make
>   A footstool of their enemies, I now take
>   You seriously in this regard…

[KEVIN rises, sits on chair, side-on to audience. Rings bell.]

> With all the enemies I can recall
> I should have enough to fill a hall!

[TWO ENEMIES enter, heads bowed in craven submission. They shuffle forward and kneel at KEVIN's feet, as his quite literal footstool.]

> How comfortable it is to see
> My once proud bitter enemies
> Baring their necks to me as they should
> For daring to challenge the divinely Good.

[KEVIN bends down to hear the appeals of forgiveness from his TWO ENEMIES present.]

> What's that? You're pleading for forgiveness now
> In Our Blessed Saviour's name,
> After all you've done to me
> Have you no sense of shame?

[Listens again.]

> 'Seventy times seven' you cry
> (Quote such scripture if you durst)…
> You've lucked out, fellows, I'm afraid
> This is your *four-hundred and-ninety first!*

[Lights down on scene, presented as a tableau. All exit, lights up. KEVIN is at his desk, sorting papers, he looks up, leans forward intently.]

> First thing on my shopping-list
> Is something my predecessors missed.
> It was Milton, I think, way back then,
> Condemned the role of those faceless men
> Called 'factions'… Yep, in *Paradise Lost!*
> How true that is I know to my cost.

> By the time I've finished having my say,
> All factions will have had their day.
> No faceless men, no *Mafiosi*,
> Will ever in future put an end to me.

[Projection of enlarged image of Holbein's portrait if King Henry VIII on screen behind KEVIN, as KEVIN stands arms similarly folded.]

> Yep I'll be Henry the Ninth, and so,
> King of the Pops! And double-woe
> To any bod like Sir Thomas More
> Who dares to differ or deplore.

[Roll of drums off-stage.]

> I'll be deaf to any Party dissent,
> An almightily righteous President.

[KEVIN walks slowly to and fro, stoking chin.]

> As for the election, I'll keep the media guessing
> (Some will be No-ing and other busily Yes-ing),
> While the *üntermensch* in a growing queue
> Await my decision and when I do
> Finally announce the election date
> They'll vote me back with that feeling you have
> When you're lost and switch on your satellite-nav…
> Popularity's now the name of the game
> And when I'm elected there'll be more of the same.

[KEVIN sits down again, leans back, relaxed, hands behind head.]

> Yes, it's all too complicated for most *them*,
> Simple offspring of Japhet, Ham, and Shem.

[Lights down. Confused noise offstage of journalist voices pestering TONY ABBOTT. Lights up on TONY being interviewed by JOURNALIST.]

JOURNALIST: Mr Abbott, Prime Minister Rudd is always referring to you as 'Captain Negative'. How do you answer that charge?

TONY: He's the Pink-Batts Man, the man who hops
Hither and yon for photo-ops,
The man whose mouth might better cope
If somebody washed it out with soap.

JOURNALIST: Yes, but your critics are shouting aloud
That all of your policies are under a cloud.

TONY: No, no, I'm afraid you've got it all wrong.
You're singing there Kevin Rudd's oldest song!
When Labour decides just when to call
The election, well then, we'll tell them all.
And then at so very late a date
There'll be very little time for much debate.

JOURNALIST *[getting frustrated]*: Yes, yes, but surely don't you see: This is what they mean by NEGATIVITY!

TONY: Patience, my friend, is all you need.
All our possums will *then* be freed…

JOURNALIST: *[scribbling furiously]* Possums, huh? Gee, thanks Mr Abbott.

TONY *[shaking head wryly]*: Metaphors! Gotta kick that habit.

[JOURNALIST winks to audience, exits. TONY stands scratching head, then exits. Lights down.]

Act Two

[Lights up. KEVIN enters, addresses audience.]

KEVIN: As a survivor from the Kokoda track
– That kind of courage I'll never lack.
Should our nation's outlook ever seem dismal
My very presence will prove charismal.
That's why I've got this appeal for youth
Who will, by way of the polling-booth,
Out-vote those grey nomadic few
Who frown at some of the things I do.
Yes, God bless the young folk on polling-day
Who'll rock and roll the blues away!

[Enter ROCK-AND-ROLL DUO, who dance on singing and jazzing around. They wear 'KEVIN-07' T-shirts and red wristbands.]

DUO: Ooh-ooh, aah-aah-aah!
Kevin's our brand-new super-star!
He's got that twinkle in his eye
Makes all our worries go 'bye-bye'!
When Kev walks into the room,
The air's electric, our hearts go boom!

He's our X-factor, he's our Guy
Sebastian makes us wanna jump and cry:
Ooh-ooh, aah-aah-aah!
Kevvie's our triple A comeback superstar!

He's Mr Cool, the great Gee Whizz!
He's just about everywhere there is!
When he's at the mike then we all know
Kevin is revvin' and rarin' to go!

Ooh-ooh, aah-aah-aah!
Wherever Kevin is, hey, there *we* are!

[DUO exit left, still singing. KEVIN smiles, shakes head sadly, reflecting on the illusions of the many.]

KEVIN: It's the speed of this modern age, I reckon
It's those great big possible futures that beckon,
The looks on young folk who'll cry and beg
For whatever their haunting dreams may call
 – It's the sight of that green light there on West Egg
Before Great Gatsby's fall.
Yep, technology's the mystic witch who'll get
Every wannabe in, for sure,
And the games they're now playing on the internet
Will be *nothing* to what's in store!

[KEVIN switches now to his personal future.]

But, for me there's a formal crowning ahead,
When *[sweeping gesture]* to all of Oz it will be known
That once more they'll be brightly led
By their rightful king on his throne.

[KEVIN suddenly freezes, struck by a fearful thought.]

Yet, why do I sometimes feel the chilling breath
Of that troubled king Shakespeare called 'Macbeth'?

[Spectral image of MALCOLM TURNBULL appears on screen.]

Why is it, sometimes, barely out of sight,
The ghost of Malcolm haunts me late at night?
What if those Libs get smart and decide to swap
Poor Tony for rich Malcolm (a fair cop!)
Malcolm's 'modest wisdom' may be a 'prop'
But those 'king-becoming graces' could well mean

> Damage to my streamlined image-machine,
> The panel-beaters have beaten out the dents
> Of the past, but I can see despite my power
> (When the powers above put on their instruments)
> I could still be written off in my finest hour.

[KEVIN nods decisively.]

> Let me think on't, as the Bard would say,
> Lest these night-fears usurp the livelong day.

[KEVIN exits, deep in thought. Scoreboard on screen: JULY OPINION POLL: ALP 50%: OPPOSITION 50%: KEVIN waves at screen, smiling.]

KEVIN: In those polls I'm level-pegging with poor Tony;
I'll use all my finesse to get it right.
Those years of backing and filling, all that phony
Stepping around assassins; every night
And day I played that game and kept my 'cool',
It's paid off big, but the biggest game's ahead:
When will I call the election? I'd be a fool
To go too soon.. Yes, when all's done and said
It's too close to the final bell to get it wrong.
The ball is in my hands, I must shoot straight.
Tony can jump and wave his arms around, so long
As he doesn't trap the ball, (or I don't make,
When shooting, some super-sized mistake).
But then there are those other powers
More particularly ours....

[KEVIN is angry frustration, walking backwards and forwards across stage.]

> Factions, factions, factions,
> It all comes down to factions!
> Who can ever safely say
> That one can guess their actions?

> They move in deep mysterious ways
> Their wonders to perform.
> In parliament you only see
> The outcome of the storm.
>
> They elsewhere plot their deep designs,
> Their policies that chill,
> And many a party leader's fate
> Depends upon their will.
>
> Behind the smiling public face
> Of factional leaders lies
> The providential power to bring
> One's swift and drear demise.
>
> With secret personal zeal they seek
> To quietly exterminate
> Their parliamentary enemies
> As Guy Fawkes did (of late).
>
> Thus Julia rose to burn me up,
> And Julia too, in turn,
> Suffered a similar fact – must I again
> On a similar pyre burn?

[KEVIN looks heavenward, hands clasped beseechingly.]

> Oh Bill, oh Kim, my good (if factional) friends!
> All ye whose wrath I've come to dread,
> Is it something I've said which angers you
>   – Or is it something I never said?

[Lights down. Lights up on OZZIE.]

OZZIE *[to audience]*: Y'know, whenever I switch the telly on
Kevin's catchin' a plane, or he's already gone...
They used to reckon if you want a job done
Ask a busy man... Well, that son-of-a-gun
Is busy as a hive of honey-bees
Or a mangy dog with a hide full of fleas,
But when you look back at what happened before
If it's more of the same we don't want any more,
But, there he is on his way again!
737 Kevin, come sunshine or rain!

[KEVIN is clearly at airport, dressed for departure.]

KEVIN: Yes-yes, I know what the papers say:
'THIRTY-FOUR FLIGHTS IN THIRTY FOUR DAYS!'
The thing is: travelling looks good,
It's big-time stuff; in fact, I would
Be off tomorrow without a care
– It's a special thing, just being there.
Only a lunatic would stay at home
With exotic otherwheres to roam.
Parliament itself is O so dreary,
A place of rest for the travel-weary.
But, if I'm out of places to roam in,
I'm like that indefatigable Roman,
My favourite Emperor, Justinian,
Who expressed his enforceable opinion
On just about everything, control
Was more central to him than his soul
(And here's a thought to move you to tears:
Justinian ruled for thirty-eight years!).
Micromanaging's also my shot,
And that explains just why I'm not
As popular as that red-haired dame
Who preceded me (what was her name?

> How easy it often is to forget
> Someone who is no longer a threat…).
> But now and then my memory,
> Like my temper, can get the better of me.

[KEVIN consults watch, frowns.]

> But look, I'm now off to Afghanistan
> Where Thérèse and I will bravely man
> Body-armour – it'll look good
> And so the bloody hell it should!
> But 'bombs away' and all that stuff,
> Politicking can get pretty rough.

[KEVIN exits quickly, smiling and waving.]

Act Three

[Enter TONY with his exercise bike. He stands before it, one hand on handlebars, facing audience.]

TONY: I think I shoulda been a bit easier on Julia.
She made me look much better by being there
(When it came to putting her foot in it, she had flair).
I was coasting, I didn't need to pedal hard,
Or get up in the stirrups… Then a peculiar
Thing happened: she was dumped. And there, recycled,
Was Kevin 07 again. That really jarred
Me almost off the track. With his changes galore
To policies he'd supported three years before
(Like the carbon tax, oh, and those faceless men
He was swearing now would never have power again),
And there, as simple as your ABC, his new alphabet
Included PNG!

[JOE HOCKEY enters, smiling, puts comforting arm around TONY.]

JOE: Don't worry, mate,
Our plans are big
– We'll have them ready
In half a jig.
Sooner or later
People will see
Through the waffle of
Mr Celebrity.

[TONY gets on bike, starts pedalling slowly, clearly still very concerned.]

TONY: I know it's just a pre-election 'fix'
But will people ever see through Kevin's tricks?
I used to worry about black holes in the road

> But it's all these roadside bombs he plans to explode
> That are slowing me down right now. To my Party backers
> I'm the cabin boy with his pocket full of crackers!

JOE *[laughing]*: Humour at this stage
> Is always welcome,
> But, cheer up mate,
> If things get worse
> We can always call on Malcolm…

[Enter MALCOLM, smiling politely.]

MALCOLM: Excuse me, folks, did someone mention my name?

[TONY and JOE look at each other.]

TONY and JOE *[together]*: 'Lo, Malcolm. We – we're very glad you came.

MALCOLM *[still smiling]*: My children, if they're home, watch *Home and Away.*
> There are hugs aplenty, glares, and lots of tears,
> And every night somebody overhears
> Private conversations where two people frown or shout
> While trying to sort themselves or their best friends out.

[MALCOLM pauses, finger on cheek.]

> I wonder just how I entered your conversation
> Could it have been because of the 'state of the nation'?

TONY *[placatory]*: Well we're all in this together, wouldn't you say?

JOE: And that jolly election gets closer every day.

TONY: You know I beat you in *our* caucus vote by one.
> Thinking about it still isn't very much fun.

MALCOLM *[still smiling]*: Of course, and I too have had to live with that.

TONY: Malcolm, we agree, but who will bell the Cheshire cat?

MALCOLM: Ah yes, I'm pleased you remembered to mention that.
I've my own views on how we should deal with Kevin.

JOE: If we could only jet-rocket him up to heaven…

TONY: Huh. He thinks he's already there. Next thing you know
He'll be telling old St Peter just where to go.

JOE: You're a good Catholic, Tony. You'd let him in.
Unless you could land him with some unforgiveable sin

[MALCOLM begins shaking his head in mock sorrow.]

    Such as telling the truth twice in a row,
    Or remembering no party's a one-man show.

[TONY, JOE AND MALCOLM nudge each other, Exit laughing. Lights up. KEVIN enters, studying a large calendar thoughtfully, flipping pages as he ponders.]

KEVIN: I've an election date – with Destiny…
Oh, if only that redoubtable She
Would openly show herself to me!

[Curtain twitches. EARLY AUGUST BLONDE peeps alluringly around left stage curtain holding 'EARLY AUGUST' sign. KEVIN notices, moves tentatively towards her.]

    Is Early August your sweet name,
    When I will sanctify my fame
    (Or consequently cop the blame)?

[EARLY AUGUST BLONDE disappears quickly as Kevin approaches.]

    Or is it late in August when
    I've got the momentum back again
    And imposed on all my regimen?

[Head of LATE AUGUST BRUNETTE appears from right stage curtain holding 'LATE AUGUST' sign. KEVIN moves more promptly towards her and addresses her.]

> Your brunette looks entice me now
> To offer you my solemn vow
> That, should be you be my optimum Thou,
> I'll win your beauteous hand – somehow.

[KEVIN pauses, gives situation further thought.]

> September, still, has some appeal –

[SEPTEMBER REDHEAD appears fully on stage holding 'SEPTEMBER' sign, wiggling bountiful hips, ogling KEVIN. KEVIN, more eagerly, moves towards her.]

> September, after all, was Julia's date,

[KEVIN hesitates at sudden problems with September.]

> But the football finals there await,
> Yom Kippur too could seal my fate…
> And then there's the G20 Summit in which I plan
> To star as much as a small star can.

[SEPTEMBER REDHEAD flounces offstage, rejected. KEVIN by now, is a little disoriented, turns to audience in appeal.]

> October, then, is all that's left…
> Am I of goodly dates bereft?
> Am I trapped in the calendar's perilous cleft?

[KEVIN flaps calendar in frustration.]

> Surely a lad so keen, so deft,
> Can choose an election date which will
> All 'moral challenges' fulfil!

[KEVIN, despondent]

> Perhaps this honeymoon I planned
> Where we will wander, hand in hand,
> Is built on rather shifting sand.

[KEVIN, strikes tragic pose, waves calendar.]

> I, the heir of all the ages,
> Consulting these meretricious pages,
> Facing future times soon passed,
> Can I forestall the winter's blast?

[Lights down briefly. Lights up as KEVIN enters. Behind him on a shelf are stacked various masks. He indicates shelf as he begins to speak.]

KEVIN: Many, many, many are the masks I use,
Masks to enchant and masks to confuse…

[KEVIN then holds up various masks, tossing them aside after use.]

> The first mask is of Mr Howard
> (But please don't consider me a coward):
> A mask for the fiscal conservative
> To show I can save, as well as give.
> A mask to wear when the time seems right
> For spending like a sailor on Saturday night,
> A mask for the man for whom what he believes
> He religiously keeps well up his sleeve.
> And a mask for the man whose worshipping self
> He can easily reach from any old shelf,
> A mask for the removable carbon-tax,
> And an ETS mask when it's time to relax.
> A mask when Howard was discouraging boats,
> And a different mask now, looking for votes.
> And a happy-happy mask for Kevin PM,
> And a much sterner mask when I'm stopping Them,
> Those party members in their factional way
> Seeking to 'top' me late in the day.

[KEVIN smiling, shaking his head.]

> Keep your eyes on Mr Twinkle-toes, good folks,
> Masks are still part of any party's joke:
> If I happen to fly to PNG
> Where masks are part of the currency
> It's not because I'm the kind of vulture
> Who wants to identify with their culture.
> But I'm a 'Choca Soldier' now
> Like those who, in the war,
> Grateful for fuzzy wuzzy mates
> Shook many a dusky paw.
> If the PNG solution doesn't work – that's tough,
> But if it's good until the election – that's enough!
> If so, and if I'm taken to task
> Back home, then there's always the ultimate mask.

[KEVIN reaches down, pretends to put on the final one, the familiar back-home one.]

> Which, thanks to the greedier media, you see
> Is…the mask of my great pop-ular-itee!

[KEVIN stares at the heap of masks.]

> If only somehow I could disconnect
> This whole 24/7 business without end
> From the part of me that's father, husband, friend,
> Those central parts of me I must protect
> Against this media-cycle. There, where love
> Can be itself, where I can, without fear,
> Respond, reach out, receive in terms that prove
> Beyond the daily venues there is here,

[KEVIN taps his chest.]

> An electorate which, if *it* were lost,
> Would mock whatever I might hope to win
> In this political bear-pit where the cost
> Of winning (whether with or without 'spin')
> Could never atone for what had been forsaken
> *Within*, where the ultimate personal vote is taken.

[KEVIN looks up now, addressing the audience.]

> Not one of us, I'm sure you will agree,
> Fits that neat media slot called 'politician';
> There's a certain common bond between us three,
> (Julia, Tony and myself), in our condition
> We seem quite puzzled at times, as though
> Our background makes uneasy our position,
> While learning, as all must, the way to go,
> These hesitations haunt us, troubling those
> Who demand that leaders show what leaders should:
> That clear confidence which the voters chose
> To lead them together towards the common good,
> Stepping firmly, of course (if we only could!),
> Not hesitating too long in a darkening wood.

[Lights down as KEVIN exits slowly. Lights up on OZZIE in usual place facing TV.]

OZZIE: Yeah, the air's chockablock with you-beaut words
Like the sea is full of boats,
And they're all a matter of great concern
Until they've got your votes.
'Compassion's' the buzz word here right now
(Like bananas when they're in season),
If you're passionate about 'compassion'
You don't need any other reason.
I mean, we all like to think we're compassionate
Like the fruit that we fancy is ripe,

On this whole immigration question
We're getting' a load of tripe.
Those bleedin' hearts are just loaded
And lookin' for somebody to accuse
And God help you, mate, if you hesitate
To share their compassionate views.
There is hardly a mention of the airports
Where they can fly into good old Oz
… Oh no, those who come in rotten old boats
They're the ones they're harpin' on 'cos
They're the ones we can see every day on the telly,

[Waves arms at TV screen.]

Of them we're always gettin' an eyeful,
But the ones with more money are able to book
Their seats on planes by the skyful!
But the other poor buggers stuck in the queue
Just don't have the money these others now do.
Queue-jumpin's OK by boat or by flight
But it wouldn't work in the city on a Saturday night.
Now Kevin and Tony are at it again
Stretchin' their vote-hungry jaws:
'You can talk of your tent city on Manus,
Mine on Nauru's still bigger than yours!'
Y'know, between the lot of us
Where everyone's ready to fight,
Would we even be havin' a discussion like this
If all of those comin' were….white?

[Lights down on OZZIE.]

Act Four

[Lights up on KEVIN who enters hurriedly, papers in hand. He is very tense and anxious.]

KEVIN: Then there's that corruption case that rocked the nation
Where Eric and his mates are in the gun,
I think I've sorted out the fumigation
And the courts will handle whatever was left undone.
Now, I'm every bit as harsh as any pollie
(The unforgivable mistake is being caught)
In condemning those who've made this melancholy
Boo-boo, it behoves us now, in deed and thought,
To brush the mud away and take full credit
For cleaning up New South (oops! I nearly said it!)
The full force of the law should be imposed
… As far as I'm concerned, the case is closed…

[KEVIN takes out mobile phone, speaks to Bill (Shorten).]

Look here, Bill, a summit's now in order
Where we can talk to people-smugglers, man to man.
Let's make it then on some distant border,
But let's make it soon (or sooner) if we can!

[Several people-smugglers enter, in rough clothes and beards. They stand in front of KEVIN, backs to the audience.]

Gentleman, if you've negative thoughts of me,
Just blame them on the weather,
Let's look at this matter optimistically:
We're all in this together!
In this problematical universe,
So full of blustering blether,
You've doubtless found, for better or worse,

> We're all in this together!
> So what if the clouds are ominous
> And we're at the end of our tether?
> All these boat-folk depend on us:
> We're all in this together!
> Why don't we unify our goals
> (The frontal and the nether)
>
> This would convince any doubtful souls
> That…we're all in this together!

[Silence. After waiting patiently for a positive response from the people-smugglers there are a few covert chuckles. Silence. Then people-smugglers leave. KEVIN stands there, hands half-raised, as if to say: What can you do? KEVIN exits. Lights down. Lights up on two rows of politicians and other concerned citizens. The ROWERS are sitting down, making rowing motions, and singing…]

ROWERS: Slow, slow, slow the boats,
> To accommodate the latest schemes
> How can we all of us pull together
> With so many different dreams?

[ROWERS pause for rest, then begin rowing again, more slowly.]

> No, no, the location of votes
> Is terribly hard to guess,
> If only, if only, if only,
> We could come up with a 'Yes'…

[ROWERS now begins rowing more vigorously.]

> Row, row, row, these boats
> To safely-distanced shores…
> Tents, tents, tents, tents,
> Mine are bigger than yours!

[A fight breaks out among the rowers. It continues as lights go down. Lights up on OZZIE. He is reading his newspaper. Shortly, he throws it down in disgust.]

OZZIE: Bugger me, if they aren't onto smokes, again…
I gave 'em away, can't remember when,
But lo and behold, better grab those packs;
Cos we're gonna be hit now with a cigarette tax.

[Large Australian flag is on screen behind speaker as PRO-SMOKING SPRUIKER enters. He is dressed as a spruiker, bow-tie, etc. Addresses audience with earnest voice.]

PRO-SMOKING SPRUIKER: Light up some fags for your country,
Start smoking them now,
Lots of you younger Australians
Will be able to show you how…

This is your patriotic duty
To which you must curtsy and bow
With chain-smoking as a monetary policy.
Our surplus you will endow.

Let every thoracic annexe
Welcome you, all cheering 'Wow!'
Each of you there on your trolley,
You are fruit for the government's bough.

Diggers once fought to defend us,
Your fags are your side-arms right now,
You're fighting to defeat that deficit,
And the civvies will shout 'Lucky cow!'

Plain packaging henceforth is treason,
Its grim warnings we now disallow,
The more that you choke on your filters,
The more you are honouring your vow.

In parliament and also in Treasury,
Your sacrifice will be honoured (somehow),
So smoke up to return us to surplus!

[PRO-SMOKING SPRUIKER gives an ironic smile as he ends the last verse.]

Here endeth my little pow-wow! Pow-wow!

Act Five

[Enter KEVIN, eagerness in his stride, smiling gently. Behind him is a large sign reading, 'VOTE FOR KEVIN ON SEPTEMBER SEVEN'! He shadow-boxes for a moment.]

KEVIN *[puffing]*: I'm as fit for this battle as I'll ever be!
        For these are uncharted waters now we're sailing
        … There's Alby and Chris who've done little amiss,
        But some of the new crew are baling…

    Oh I'm keenly aware there'll be journos who swear
    That we're all now aboard the *Titanic*,
    With icebergs galore both aft and before
    And visible signs of a panic,

    But one word to the crew, a veiled threat or two,
    And my confidence (just short of manic)
    Will settle them down and success will crown
    A campaign which will be talismanic!

    The number 7, you see, will be lucky for me,
    With old Tony hang-dog like a dingo,
    While I'll be still bright as a light on that night
    When they call my number in BINGO!

    I'll be underdog-modest, the best of disguises
    No arrogant poses you'll see,
    Any capital sins will be slipped into bins
    … The Seven Gifts of the Spirit for me!

    When questions are asked about national debt
    Budget deficit, Gonski, Nauru,
    Such questions I will greet with demeanour so sweet
    That every doubter (yes, even you)

Will put aside all of my past you recall,
The policies you felt were inane,
In the ultimate truth of the polling-booth
You'll vote me back as your PM again!

[Lights down. KEVIN is seated at a small table, nibbling at some healthy snacks while talking to his close friend, JOHN. A newspaper lies open on the table next to KEVIN.]

KEVIN: I see they're now calling me
A bit of a Machiavel,
After that Italian prince
That, I gather, did so well…

JOHN: Kevin, it's the fate of all of us sooner
Or later in public life,
And much harder in fact to disprove than those claims
That you're still beating your wife.

KEVIN: I know that the Elizabethans
Plugged that line
That Machiavel was every ill
That they could ever define…

JOHN: Well, Italy way back then
Was a series of competing states
(Something that every federalist
In Canberra loves and hates).

KEVIN: But was he as wicked and scheming
As a lot of them still say?

JOHN *[laughing]*: No, but he was healthily cynical
In a very modern way,
Which he thought would ensure a ruler
Who was in, was there to stay.

KEVIN *[with increasing interest]*: Now that's what I'd like to happen
　　　　　　　　Here in my case,
　　　　　　　　When they throw these words like 'Machiavel"
　　　　　　　　Up in my own face…

JOHN:　　　　To be hated or to be feared
　　　　　　　Which was worse?
　　　　　　　If one didn't win you support
　　　　　　　Then the reverse!
　　　　　　　Over-confidence could lead
　　　　　　　To public distrust
　　　　　　　But not to be hated, but *feared*
　　　　　　　That was a 'must!'
　　　　　　　Remember the effective leader should always
　　　　　　　Seem to possess
　　　　　　　Qualities to which the people would
　　　　　　　Give a resounding 'Yes'.

KEVIN:　　　Hmmnn. Compassion's a big question here
　　　　　　　In our country right now
　　　　　　　With this illegal immigrant question,
　　　　　　　I'm just wondering how….

JOHN:　　　　The leader should be a man of good faith
　　　　　　　And also integrity
　　　　　　　(Or, to say the very least,
　　　　　　　He should *appear* to be).

　　　　　　　A good leader, Machiavel said,
　　　　　　　Should generally know
　　　　　　　That the balance of fear and respect
　　　　　　　Is the best way to go;

　　　　　　　To be as as a lion
　　　　　　　When a lion's power is required,
　　　　　　　And as cunning as a fox when respect
　　　　　　　Is also to be desired.

[KEVIN, thoughtfully munching, rises from seat, shaking hands warily with JOHN.]

KEVIN: Thanks very much, John,
                  For making it very clear
                  That there's still plenty of room
                  For a Machiavel right here!

[KEVIN and JOHN exit, KEVIN'S arm in a friendly way around John's shoulder. Lights down. TONY enters, looks upset at poster which says in bold letters 'VOTE 1 TONY FOR STABLE GOVERNMENT'.]

TONY *[stroking chin]*: September, hey? What then?
                  Everybody says it's Us or Them.
                  It's black and white…No, hang on a minute!
                  Those Greens and Indies are still in it.
                  They could swing the voting Kevin's way
                  (Or mine). In either case we all will pay
                  A hefty price (like poor Julia did, twice).
                  Both Kevin and I will work to see it doesn't happen,
                  But like giant termites I can hear them tappin',
                  And many a house that looked secure and good
                  Will eventually crumble away into rotten wood.
                  In which case we will suffer the sort of pain
                  Of winding up with a hung parliament, again.

[TONY exits deep in thought. Enter KEVIN. He is singing and dancing. He is dressed in a surgeon's green 'scrubs'.]

KEVIN: In my previous incarnation
                  I may have got a few things wrong:
                  Pink batts, and carbon tax, and mounting debt
                  Delivered quite a pong,
                  But in my re-incarnated self
                  I'm singing a different song.
                  It's the New Way, to face a brand-new future,

It's the New Way we guarantee will suit ya.
For now I am the surgeon for this body politic,
Adept at snake-oil remedies for anyone who's sick.
I've a suture for the future that still has yet to happen
In 2025 (unless again we're busy nappin').
It's the New Way, distinguishable from the old
As clearly as your whooping-cough is different from your cold.
You see behind me now (though carefully out of sight)
My new advisor team who're still unaccustomed to the light,
In the newness of the new you may at first have a bit of doubt
But the familiarity of the new will most surely trickle out.
Would I be saying this, my friends, if it were less than true,
Since you know me as certainly as I, in fact, know you…?

[KEVIN dances offstage right, still singing. MAN and WOMAN enter, smile at each other (they've met before). They face the audience and speak in blank verse.]

WOMAN: More keenly than most other creatures, we
            Become aware of our own transience
            And struggle in so many ways to give
            Our temporary residence at times the feel,
            The look, the shape, the permanence of home.

MAN *[nodding]*: Oh, I agree, those Altamira caves, Lascaux,
            And many more recent such are tributes to
            Our longing to inscribe on rocks, with rocks
            Such as Stonehenge, our still stubbornly blunt
            Determination to at least endure
            In the memories of others what we were…

WOMAN: And what we are, as well. Those Neolithic lives
            Had complications as profoundly real
            As any we now face, and while we argue
            About our own climatic destiny we should
            Always do what we can to remember theirs.

MAN: We excavate a tunnel and discover
Earth's history written in the very act
Of building our own future...

WOMAN: Yes, all our mining
Reminds us of the past. I think, at times
(Especially now as the often tedious hinges
Of our political mentors' tongues
Creak desperately in the wind, the short-term gain
Tending to obscure the long-term pains).

MAN: I couldn't agree more. We let the land
Be mined to within an inch of its life and even dream
Of settlement elsewhere should our life here
On this planet be no longer sustainable.

WOMAN *[nodding]*: Our seas and rivers too have felt the weight
Of exploitation from the first. Then, as well,
Towns shrivel while those ever-greater
Conurbations we call 'cities' struggle
To accommodate the drift which steals away,
Like high tides do, the very things which made
Them habitable. Not since World War II
Have so many homeless happened, here as elsewhere,
Depending on the sympathy of others.

MAN: Then, too, the burgeoning drug-culture will ensure
That many who for many reasons fall
Into its talons and sophistications
Will certainly be lost. We're often amazed
On the news to learn of the numerous raids
On modest suburban premises fitted out
As factories for the tragic trades pursued.

WOMAN: And then they dare to tell us all is well.
We're healthy while so many thousands suffer
And cause suffering to others, as though this can be blinked
Out of existence by those bold assertions
Politically inspired to lull us all
Into a sense of false security.

MAN: Indeed, those current affairs programmes reveal
How many people too now happily trash
Government-funded houses simply because
They can. So also, nightly, we may witness
Via security cameras that violence
We think can never happen to us, so digitally aware,
So coolly modern, so inescapably dumb.

WOMAN: Oh yes, I think our political masters,
Should, (as policeman once could afford to)
Patrol a regular electorate beat like policemen did,
And not just door-knock in election years. Kevin said
He door knocked 38,000 homes – a bid
For the Guinness Book of Records, seemingly!

[WOMAN and MAN stand, arms spread in a shrug. Lights down. Lights up. OZZIE enters, with newspaper, which he tosses on chair. He remains standing, as if finally saying his piece.]

OZZIE: Mullin' over this election,
Now that we've got a date,
I've been battlin' to sum up, in my head
How the two leaders rate.
They call Kevin 'Mr Zippy',
You can sit there in your chair
… Just switch the telly on… Hello!
Mr Zippy's there.
He looks so very charmin'
He's over you like a rash.

Poshed up and quite disarmin'.
With that Presidential dash,
He's got a swag of promises
(Includin' some that he might keep).
But if you're among the Doubtin' Thomases
You'd better not go to sleep.
His smile's still toothpaste friendly,
His greetin's well *[searches for word] verbose*,
But those who know him reckon
You should watch him very close:
Because another Kevin's waitin'
Behind that kitchen door
Whose mood's *[searches again for word] exacerbatin'*
And whose manners you'd deplore.

[OZZIE now sits down, relaxed, smiling.]

While Tony, he's the sort of bloke
You'd be happy to ask to tea,
He's no bloody astronaut,
He's more like you and me.
He doesn't come in bubble-wrap,
Self-love is not his thing,
He's often kind of tentative,
But there's no hidden sting.
I'd say he's a team-man basically,
He's all that Kevin's not,
Not bustin' a gut just to impress:
What you see is what you got.
Yeah, he's no dumb Narcissus
In love with his reflection,
And that's another reason why
Tony could win this election.

> But in the media-world of buzz-and-click
> Where reality's image-driven,
> How can you tell real fur from fake,
> And the giver from the given?
> Campaign's just a thing apart
> … It's the footie-stars visitin' schools
> But government is the real game's heart
> And it's played by different rules.

[OZZIE pauses, remembering his working days.]

> Where I worked, we had a boss
> All smiles and lots of palaver
> But when things went wrong he turned into
> A butcher with a carver.
> In Canberra they generally get
> This one B.A. degree
> By feeding us mushrooms in the dark
> With Bullshit Artistry.

[He shakes his head, chuckling as Lights down. Offstage knocking becomes ever louder. Three Green politicians enter. They are all wearing articles of green in different shades. Their leader, GREEN ONE, is a woman. She addresses both KEVIN and TONY.]

GREEN ONE: Remember us? We thought you would.
>> We've been here before.
>> We'll hold the balance of power again,
>> Perhaps even a little bit more…

GREEN TWO: We're interested in lots of things,
>> Not just hugging trees.

GREEN THREE: Some say we are the kind of cure
>> That's worse than the disease…

GREEN ONE: Remember once when polio
    Was such a worldwide curse
    And much of the medical profession
    Went crook at our bush nurse?
    Sister Kenny was her name
    (A Queensland girl, that's true)
    Who said that binding up a limb
    Wasn't the best that we should do?

[GREEN TWO and GREEN THREE nod vigorously in agreement.]

GREEN TWO: That's right! Elizabeth Kenny thought
    That the muscle and the brain
    Could work together to liberate
    The affected part again.

GREEN THREE *[eagerly]*: And that's also in many ways
    What we intend to do,
    And that's why we're offering the power
    To rule to *one of you.*

[All three GREENS nod and stand, arms extended towards KEVIN and TONY. KEVIN, a little startled, recovers quickly, and responds by opening his arms to embrace all three, if that's physically possible. TONY, however, appears indifferent to their appeal.]

KEVIN: Unaccustomed as I am to being flattered,
    Now, when every source of support has mattered,
    I may, as Julia did when in my place,
    Welcome you to my (relatively) warm embrace…

[All three GREENS rush to be hugged. However, KEVIN's embrace is clearly circumstantial and lacks warmth.]

    However, I do recall in those past times
    President Roosevelt instituted the March of Dimes…

[Here the GREENS freeze, as the history of President Rooseveldt's support for a fund from the American people enabled new medical alternatives such as the Salk vaccine and the Sabine injection to reduce dramatically the need for Sister Kenny's method.]

> And then in due course came Salk vaccine and Sabine
> That changed what that word 'polio' could mean.
> Thereafter, Sister Kenny's valuable treatment lost its allure
> So your support may not be required as a cure.

[Here KEVIN pushes the GREENS further away and stands, hands folded, magisterially, now addressing the audience over the heads of the GREENS.]

> Alas, my children, here I may then follow
> Julia Whats-er-name (I beat her hollow)
> What was her name? For the love of me I can't remember,
> But I've still got to beware of the Ides of September.

[Lights down, as GREENS stand, huddled together, watching KEVIN and TONY leave. Lights up. KEVIN is about to use his mobile phone to ring various past leaders of the ALP in an attempt to coerce them into rejoining his election team as candidates. Beside him is a large poster lettered 'RUDD RECYCLING MARKET!' which KEVIN indicates, as he speaks to audience.]

KEVIN: It's the Rudd Recycling Market here,
         My new election venture
         Has already drawn upon itself
         Our enemies' swift censure.

         We believe that we have still in stock
         Re-marketable old pollies
         … Top brands the public still may buy
         Despite their various follies.

We've already spruced up once again
A Premier who's re-tired,
As a wordy Foreign Minister,
The kind that is required,

And a beaming Premier from the North
Whose gearing later cost
Poor Anna Bligh that future
She so ruinously lost.

Peter once said nasty things
About me he wanted to say,
But *tomorrow* often sweetens the flavour
We grimaced at *yesterday*.

Myself, I was once a vehicle
That was taken off the road,
But now that I'm also back again
Would like to share the load

With other has-been machines which
Although in no sense new,
May, by my deft recycling
Still appeal to you.

I'll be on the phone in a moment
To Gough and Bob and Paul
To be part of this heaven-sent market
Which may benefit us all!

Why, even Mark (God spare the mark!)
May, with new wheels and brakes,
Help us to win another seat
(Despite occasional shakes…).

> Like the *Malvern Star* they've had their day
> But the names still ring a bell
> Recycling may be just the thing
> To save us all from *[gulps]* Hell!
>
> Who knows? You folk out there may well
> Have other brands in mind
> (Like Kim…or even Simon (no,
> *He'd* best be left behind…).
>
> Remember this recycling shed *[waves arm to indicate shed]*
> Is open at all hours,
> Lest we, like Mr Wordsworth,
> May, too, lay waste our powers…

[As he leaves stage KEVIN is ringing Gough on his mobile phone.]

> I wonder if by any chance
> (Please excuse this cough)
> I might just have a word or two
> With my old cobber Gough?

[Exit KEVIN. Lights down.]

Act Six

[TONY is talking to BOB, political advisor, as the Lights go up. He is on his exercise bike; he continues to pedal thoughtfully throughout most of the discussion.]

TONY: I thought I'd better get a bit of coaching;
Kevin's setting such a hectic pace
I've been pedalling away for years,
But I can't help feel he's poaching
The limelight and I want to win this race.

BOB: Yeah, right. With Julie there
You looked bound to win
(She was hardly the world's champion
When it came to handling 'spin').

TONY: They reckon easy pedalling's out for me
What do you think could be the remedy?

BOB: They're quite right, you know.
Full speed ahead, now, Tony, that's the only way to go.

TONY: I've been too long just coasting down the hill.

BOB: You've got a better track-time than *him* still.

TONY *[nodding]*: When you're in a race you've got to keep an eye
On the competition or they'll pass you by.

BOB: Exactly. You've been around a bit, and you're a better politician
And you know that all this jostling for position
Is what the media love, but just remember
It's a day-in, day-out bike race till September!
It's time to strike back now. Your biggest asset
If your unblemished record. You're a basset

	-hound while he's a yapping little poodle,

              -hound while he's a yapping little poodle,
              Or like the kid in class who still prefers to doodle
              An image of himself as Abraham Lincoln
              With an ink-well that he's never put any ink in.

TONY: Kevin comes up well on telly and the papers…

BOB: And that'll just remind folks of the capers
              He got up to before by spending bigger
              Than he could ever reasonably figger!

[Becoming even more serious now.]

              Look, you're a better man than he is, Gungha Din,
              Loosen up a little and you'll win,
              Hit back at him with policies; he's a liar,
              And like fire-fighters do: fight fire with fire.
              … That'll set him back a peg or two, okay?

TONY *[dismounting from bike]*: Thanks a lot, Bob,
              Now I see the way
              To burn him off…

BOB: Remember what I say:
              A steady punishing course, just like I said,
              And when the opinion polls catch up, he's as good as dead!

[Lights down. Both exit. KEVIN enters at stage right. He is wearing a white shirt. He rolls up his sleeves revealing heavily tattooed arms.]

KEVIN: I am the Illustrated Man
              One who hasn't his past out-ran
              Look closely now and you will see
              All of my political past on me.
              Tattooed am I from head to toe,
              My past is with me wherever I go
              Once I was known as 'Dr Death'

(They say it now with bated breath).
They are those parts of me I'd wish away;
And yet, it seems, they're here to stay.

I've tried to burn them off, tried acid, knife,
But still they are part of my public life.
If only I could really rub them out
Voters then would have little doubt,
But those deeds move when my lips move,
Reminding those who know me well
That there is always more to tell.

Cartoonists treat me as a joke,
I smile at children, hug old folk
I meet whenever I choose to speak
But beneath this skin some think I'm weak,

Weak as the policies I pronounce…
'We've seen him yesterday,' they say,
'He caused us many a grief before
When he came a-knocking at our door.'

I do whatever a doomed man can,
I dance, glad-hand, and wave to all,
But still these tattoos will recall
The ruinous schemes I've introduced:

Carbon tax, BER, pink batts,
The immigration cock-up that's
Still twitching as I move about…
(A tattoo I could do without)
O pity me now, if you still can,

For I am your Illustrated Man.

[It is late at night. Lights are subdued, as is KEVIN. He is alone and reflecting on his defeat.]

KEVIN: Who knows where all my problems started?
How far back in the past one has to go?
Could it be one of the times when I departed,
On instinct, from the same old ebb-and-flow
From those union heavyweights who put you up or down?
And yet, at times, I still wonder
If it's those policies at which the public frown
(As people do when they hear a clap of thunder,
Put up their brollies and wait for the rain to come down?)
Perhaps I just came on too strong, too soon,
And I was not that bright new sun I once had been,
But rather, like a very clouded moon
As lucky 07 became unlucky 13
('Unlucky for some!' the bingo caller cries…
Ah well, one does one's best. At least one *tries!*)

[KEVIN is still pondering this when there is a heavy knocking on the door.]

KEVIN *[startled]*: Who could it possibly be at this late hour?
Some drunken bum from that lugubrious farewell party?
Or another last-minute unexpected blow,
Now when I'm far less bright and far less hearty …
I only wish they would quietly go
Or (a terrible thought just struck me) could it
Be a Party faction with a suggestion
That I resign forthwith? Ah well, would it
Make any difference now? It's a pointless question
Now all the votes are in…

[ATTENDANT enters, concerned for KEVIN's safety.]

ATTENDANT: Some burly gentlemen, sir, with threatening actions,
                I believe they're from our major Party factions,
                Both Right and Left. They all look very serious…

KEVIN *[resignedly]*: Yes and I'm sure they're also equally imperious.

[ATTENDANT nods, exits. KEVIN shrugs, faces audience. Lights down.]

            'Unlucky for some!' the Bingo caller cries.
            Ah well, I'm not the sort that when he loses, dies.

[Lights out. KEVIN is still alone, facing the audience, facing another unpredictable future. OZZIE enters, looks ironically at his familiar TV as he advances to centre stage front to address audience.]

OZZIE: Speakin' for all the great unwashed
             Who never got near the polished or poshed,
             Worked for a living, dug ditches and stuff,
             Couldn't put a shovel down quickly enough,
             Before all this digital pizazz came along,
             When dirt and grease were still part of the song.,
             Deeper and deeper under the skin,
             We watched the pollies go out and come in,
             So it's all a bit of a sham to us
             When our place is right there in the back of the bus…
             Is it any wonder that more and more
             We're turned off, dozin', and startin' to snore?
             There are many folk out there doin' their best
             But they don't have the power, the ultimate test.
             So if this compulsory votin' went out
             Many would give a helluva shout
             (Till a future a damn sight worse came along
             Then maybe they'd be singin' a different song).
             Who cares if farmers are havin' it tough
             And the supermarkets are playin' it rough,
             So the milk and the fruit and the rest of the stuff

Includin' the shoes and the shirts we get
Are made by somebody's cheaper sweat?
And the queue of the homeless continues to grow
And how to reduce it no one seems to know,
And youth unemployment's now on the rise,
Bringin' sorrow and fear to many eyes,
And pollies talk of 'the people' as though we were static
Somethin' to switch on to as quite automatic,
But if you talk to most folk after a bit
You realise many just don't give a shit.
But look who's talkin'…it's silly old Ozzie
With no more influence than any male mozzie,
So go tell your pollie; but what'd be the use
They're too busy practising personal abuse,
Fired up by Canberra jungle juice.

[Election night, a TV studio, the vote-counting on TV has produced a sombre mood rather than the usual suspense-filled atmosphere.]

MALE COMMENTATOR ONE *[to audience]*:
>Hello, folks, we're all on our best behaviour here tonight.
>It looks like it's all over, bar the shouting.

MALE COMMENTATOR TWO:
>And that's usually be done by whoever wins the fight.

MALE COMMENTATOR THREE:
>And as to that, there's little cause for doubting.

ISABEL: Yes, this isn't like that famous Dewey-Truman show,
When Dewey for President headlines were ready to print,
And the wise guys got it wrong, so you never know…

MALE COMMENTATOR ONE:
>But we've got analysts now with a digital squint
>Can tell you, after 5% are counted,
>Who's alive, and who's a hunting trophy to be mounted.

MALE COMMENTATOR TWO:
> Well, there are some aspects, just the same
>   – Griffith, for instance, where the PM looked
> A goner at one stage, but then he came
> Good, so his goose wasn't cooked.

MALE COMMENTATOR THREE:
> If his goose wasn't cooked, it still got a helluva fright.

MALE COMMENTATOR ONE:
> Ummm… Let's look again at Corangamite
> We have a lady present you all know, called Isabel.

[Turns to ISABEL.]

> You've wined and dined the Party leaders, can you tell
> What mood you found these leaders in, given that very
> *Relaxed* environment? I mean it wasn't like Charon's ferry
> To Hades, or how some people felt on *Q & A*.

ISABEL: I'm glad you asked me that. I have to say
> I think they were immensely grateful for a chance
> To get away from the usual bear-pit thing
> (You know, staked and forced to dance
> To the yammering of dogs) and also obliged to sing.

MALE COMMENTATOR THREE:
> Ah well, that's how the lesson often ends,
> When even warnings cannot spare you.
> From the public shame to come,
> When, alas, the loss of many friends
> Must beat its truth into you like a drum,
> And you must look around to find that some,
> Even despite their foolishness, survive,
> And vow that a keener awareness in the future
> Will manage to keep more of your *friends* alive.

ISABEL *[reflectively]*: And those election posters you can see
          In your minds' eye are all now history.

[Lights down on this scene. Lights up on large screen registering the election results: 'COALITION IN: LABOUR OUT'. Enter KEVIN smiling wryly, shrugs then begins to sing.]

KEVIN *[singing]*: Oh yes, I was a Great Campaigner.
          It was something I did very well,
          I was so much in touch, I could cover so much
          (All those promises flowing pell-mell)
          But now I can hear that bell…

[A bell tolls offstage, persisting faintly throughout the rest of his song.]

          I've been out there busting my britches,
          I'm the Instant Policy Man:
          For me, new ideas are like itches,
          And I scratch them whenever I can.

[KEVIN pauses, points to bell still ringing faintly offstage.]

          That bell there has sounded for many,
          And it's ringing right now just for me
          The handshakes and back-pats have ended,
          It's "Tooroo!" to my vision so splendid,
          My campaigning is now history, history,
          There'll be no more big comebacks for me.

[In a very different mood, KEVIN solemnly addresses the audience.]

          While I have no great affinity with failure,
          As the most famous Mandarin speaker in Australia,
          Like any of those Middle Kingdom rulers of old,
          Circumstances have so loosened my firm hold
          On my imperial vision, I, now, Kevin,
          Must bow to the very same Mandate of Heaven.

[KEVIN takes out his mobile phone.]

> Hello, is that the University of Adelaide?
> Good, I wonder if I could have
> A word or two with Julia – sorry, *Professor* Gillard?
> Oh, I see. So, she's gone off *where*? *[Pause]*
> To America? Well, she'll be safer there.

[Lights down. Lights up again. Enter TRUE BELIEVER. He is wearing a Sunshine State T-shirt and suit.]

TRUE BELIEVER: If you're ever in Eumumdi
> On a Saturday or Sundee
> They'll point you to that humble farm
> Where Kevin Rudd was born,
> And if you go to Nambour
> Where the roads have better camber,
> That's where Kevin with his school-bag
> Hurried through the winter dawn.

> Yes, they'll tell you all those stories
> About his youthful glories,
> How he studied like a demon
> (He had brains he'd yet to use)
> And when he went to Brizzy
> And set everyone in a tizzy
> There they called him 'Dr Death'
> In (affectionate) abuse.

> In Canberra Kevin was a winner
> Who would often skip his dinner
> Because he had some plan for which our nation stood in need,
> While the world was all at sea
> With that thing called GFC
> Kevin saved us from that misery by spending at great speed.

Kevin's Education Revolution
Was another great solution
With a laptop for every single kid as soon as he could spell
(Sometimes, even sooner:
There's a pre-school in Laguna
Where the kindergarten nippers are in touch with Intertel!)

In Eumundi there's a statue
And it's so eye-catching that you
Will immediately bow in reverence to our Sunshine State PM;
He sits there just as proud and spry
As did Flash Jack from Gundagai,
If his bronze lips could speak they'd say: 'It's either *Us* or *Them!*'

Yes, you Southerners may well shrink,
It's much later than you think:
Where Kevin Almighty rose to fame, another Queenslander instead
Will blaze a golden track
From city to outback
And show that we have leaders, too, and you will then be led!

[TRUE BELIEVER stands with upraised fist in triumph as lights go slowly down. Lights up SAM SPINMEISTER addresses a meeting of senior ALP leaders in relation to their defeat in the Federal election.]

SAM SPINMEISTER: This meeting has been called now to consider
The way ahead for us and our great Party.

SIMON BREEN: Not so great for us, given what happened.

SAM SPINMEISTER: It's all in the way you look at it, my friend.

SIMON BREEN: Tell that to the many who's just lost their seats.

SAM SPINMEISTER: Every election comes with possible losses.
But there are certain gains that come as well.

SIMON BREEN: Such as? Just name one. I bet you can't.

SAM SPINMEISTER: It could have been much worse, remember that.

SIMON BREEN: The second biggest defeat since Federation.

SAM SPINMEISTER: But not as great as the media smarties predicted.
    So they were quite wrong there, for a start.
    Friends, we should look at this as an occasion
    From which we can take heart, the past behind us…

SIMON BREEN: So what would you call what just happened to us?

SAM SPINMEISTER: I'd call it just a 'setback', nothing more.

SIMON BREEN: Too many more setbacks like this,
    And we won't exist.

SAM SPINMEISTER: Every Party gets defeated, sooner or later.

SIMON BREEN: Look, this isn't like some TV talent show
    Complete with judges seeking Golden Logies;
    It's not the X Factor we had to have:
    It's the *Why?* factor we should be asking
    Ourselves right now!

SAM SPINMEISTER: Look, call it a disaster, if you wish.
    But not the catastrophe it could have been
    You'll see, we will be stronger for this challenge.
    The only way ahead for us is *up*.
    We're too great a Party to stay down.

SIMON BREEN: It'll be years before we're really competitive.

SAM SPINMEISTER: We're in there now. This is just Day One.
    We're all aware we've lost some good people.

SIMON BREEN: And we're still stuck with some people not so good.

SAM SPINMEISTER: Gloom, doom. Look on the bright side, pal.

SIMON BREEN: Okay, so what we've got's a temporary *setback*.
Or is it the *defeat* we had to have?
Or is it the *disaster* we saw coming?
Or is it merely a *catastrophe*, or what?
Next you'll be calling it a *victory*,
Like Hitler did the loss of Stalingrad.
You're spinning like a top, mate!
Can't you stop?

[Immediate uproar. KEVIN pops his head around door.]

KEVIN: I just happened to be passing, folks, and heard this awful din.
Is this a very domestic fight, or can anyone join in?

SIMON BREEN: Well, since you're part of the problem, mate,
We'd all be of this conclusion:
That your extra speedy departure
Would be part of the solution!

[Lights down as battle rages. OZZIE now turns, sits down facing TV. He gestures towards it, smiling.]

OZZIE: I've been watchin' pollies actin' up every day,
So they seem like endless repeats of *Home and Away*.
Where all the headline promises you get
Become tomorrow's small-print words of regret,
But look, I'm only a back-up in this show;
I've said all I want to now, so I'll let you go…

Final Curtain

www.ingramcontent.com/pod-product-compliance
Lightning Source LLC
Chambersburg PA
CBHW071037080526
44587CB00015B/2650